As a Community we are called to share the fruits of our heart journey, and the outworking of our charism and calling. One of the ways in which we do this is by publishing a number of series of booklets that explore our core teaching. These series include:

- Gold series: an expansion on our Rule of Life – the Community's core teaching.

- Green series: a look at our influences, past and present – the things that have shaped us.

- Red series: an exploration of spiritual formation and disciplines – to provide some tools for the inner journey.

These booklets are a way of developing Community life, but also a way of sharing something of the wisdom gained on our journey with people beyond the Community.

The exploration of the inner journey before God is at the heart of who we are as a Community as, in gaining understanding of ourselves, we learn how better to live with others. This booklet is part of our Gold series, exploring our core teaching.

To put each booklet in context, they all begin with a summary of our Rule of Life, the questions at our heart, and the purpose and nature of Northumbria Community.

Summary of our Rule of Life

This is the Rule we embrace. This is the Rule we will keep:
we say YES to AVAILABILITY; we say YES to VULNERABILITY.

We are called to be AVAILABLE to God and to others:

- Firstly to be available to God in the **cell** of our own heart when we can be turned towards Him, and seek His face;

- then to be available to others in a call to exercise **hospitality**, recognising that in welcoming others we honour and welcome the Christ Himself;

- then to be available to others through participation in His care and concern for them, by praying and **interceding** for their situations in the power of the Holy Spirit;

- then to be available for participation in **mission** of various kinds according to the calling and initiatives of the Spirit.

We are called to intentional, deliberate VULNERABILITY:

- We embrace the vulnerability of being **teachable** expressed in:
  - a discipline of prayer;
  - in exposure to Scripture;
  - a willingness to be accountable to others in ordering our ways and our heart in order to effect change.

- We embrace the responsibility of taking the **heretical imperative**:
  - by speaking out when necessary or asking awkward questions that will often upset the status quo;
  - by making relationships the priority, and not reputation.

- We embrace the challenge to live as church without walls, living openly amongst unbelievers and other believers in a way that the life of God in ours can be seen, challenged or questioned. This will involve us building friendships outside our Christian ghettos or club-mentality, not with ulterior evangelistic motives, but because we genuinely care.

The three questions at our heart

Northumbria Community is the gift of God to those whose hearts are set on pilgrimage and whose lives are constantly being redefined and redirected by the living out of these three questions. Companions in Community are able to help each other keep these questions alive.

- Who is it that you seek?

- How then shall we live?

- How shall we sing the Lord's song in a strange land?

Our purpose

To embody a set of values, described in our Rule of Life of Availability and Vulnerability, which echoes, and points to, the life of Christ, and to support one another in our commitment to orientate ourselves toward this as a way for living. Knowing we have named and committed ourselves to this Rule **fosters perseverance.**

To hold the truth of the paradox of the Christian journey as being one taken alone/together. Each must take the journey alone. There is no substitute for leaning our own head on the breast of Christ and listening for heartbeat of God. There is no abdicating our own responsibility for our own life and no shortcuts for the work, struggle and intimacy of the cell of the heart before God. Yet, whilst on the journey, we are together. Others are headed in the same direction and come alongside to offer encouragement. Sometimes this encouragement is direct and verbal, sometimes it is through friendship, sometimes it comes through prayer support, and sometimes it is knowing that someone else is on a similar path through the wilderness of the inner exile. Knowing we are connected to others on the journey **fosters courage.**

To inspire each other to each be our own one-of-a-kind, God-designed selves. In a culture of celebrity, consumerism and hyper-productivity, the Northumbria Community strengthens people to be themselves. Knowing we are each accepted for who we are, and accepting others for who they are, **fosters authenticity.**

To encourage each other to live the questions at the heart of our journey alone/together. No one is going to give us the answer. No one is going to show us what living this way looks likes for each of us in our own contexts. We have to risk, experiment and make peace with mystery. Living with the questions and discerning how to live the Rule in our own context **fosters creativity.**

To be a sign that another way of living is possible. Even if people are not called to be Companions with us, the living witness of an alternative way gives refreshment to those, both within and without the Church, who see and need it. Knowing there are real choices around how to live and connect **fosters hope.**

Our nature

The renewal of the church will come from a new type of monasticism which only has in common with the old an uncompromising allegiance to the Sermon on the Mount. It is high time men and women banded together to do this.

Dietrich Bonhoeffer

Dynamic and erratic, spontaneous and radical, audacious and immature, committed if not altogether coherent, ecumenically open and often experimental, visible here and there, now and then, but unsettled institutionally. Almost monastic in nature but most of all enacting a fearful hope for human life in society.

William Stringfellow

The Northumbria Community occupies an interesting 'Third Space', which is not the long established denominations or their traditional monastic communities, and nor is it a newer form of church or newer 'new monastic' community. One of the gifts of the Northumbria Community to the body of Christ today is that it is rooted through its thirty years of exploration, and yet at the same time it is also still seen to be experimental and prophetic.

John Pritchard

Preface

This booklet is part of a series of core teaching booklets that tell the story of the development of the Community's life and ethos from the persepective of the founding generation. They tell the story of the call of God to the Community's pioneers and the blessings and bewilderments of the journey they have taken in response to it over the past thirty years.

These booklets are foundation stones. They are offered as a gift to the next generations of Community Companions, for them to take and use as they move on. But they are not the last word on the subject. Instead, they can be seen as a starting point for the next phase of the Community's life and journey. They are an invitation into conversation between the generations and a provocation to the third generation and beyond to 'build the new on foundations of old'.

Each generation must reinterpret the Community's Way for Living for their own situation and within their own culture as they encounter it in everyday life. But not everything needs reinventing. At the heart of our Community's life are enduring truths and these we need to hold and to treasure, and pass on to those who come on behind us. It is these truths that we attempt to offer within the pages of these booklets. We hope that you will read and reflect on them.

Alone

Together

INTRODUCTION

The Northumbria Community is a geographically dispersed network of people, from different backgrounds, streams and edges of the Christian faith, and is now, in the second decade of the 21st century, scattered across many parts of the world.

We identify with the growing number of Christians who feel the Spirit redirecting their experience of God as expressed by:

- a concern to seek God more deeply;

- a call to repentance, and self-denial;

- a call to discerning and resisting evil;

- a call to discover and express a different way of living out our faith, identifying and engaging with our contemporary culture.

We aspire to be a Community that lives out in practice the core values of our Rule of Life as a way for living. This way for living is characterised by our desire to explore a new inner monasticism of the heart, so we can live with hope despite the inner chaos we feel as a result of the massive cultural changes we are living through. This new monasticism draws from ancient monastic wisdom; it seeks a fresh understanding of the principles that motivated those early monks, in order to live those insights as a present-day expression of 'contemplation in a world of action'.

We believe that to be alive and to stay alive to God requires us to continually embrace the vulnerability of being teachable. The Desert Fathers had a pithy saying: 'When the disciple is ready, the teacher appears.' In other words, it's only as we're open to fresh understanding in our walk with God, always learning, and always applying what we learn to life as it is, that we are taught how to 'grow in the grace and knowledge of our Lord Jesus Christ'. (2 Peter 3:18)

As Northumbria Community Companions our individual stories merge into the story God has written on each of our hearts, as his calling upon each of our lives. We are comm-unity, in that we share a common unity of vocational expression, that is:

- each (Alone) pursues relationship with God, seeking Him for Himself as our primary purpose;

- all (Together) follow a common Rule of Life, as each says 'Yes' to God through Availability and Vulnerability as a way for living;

- each of us embraces a Rhythm of Prayer (Daily Office) as the unique person we are, where we are, and what we are, in our seeking and serving God.

Whilst the detail will vary from Companion to Companion, and from one day to another, the important foundational questions at the heart of our ethos and journey remain as a constant for each of us:

- Who is it that you seek?

- How then shall we live?

- How shall we sing the Lord's song in a strange land?

The Northumbria Community is the gift of God to those whose hearts are set on this particular pilgrimage and whose lives are continuously being redefined and redirected by living out these three questions in whatever situation or circumstance we find ourselves. Being covenanted together in such varied ways, we endeavour to play our part in 'enacting a fearful hope for society'.

> We are pilgrims on a journey and Companions on the road
> We are here to help each other, walk the mile and bear the load.

These are the themes we will shape and develop in this booklet.

Chapter 1

Alone Together:
a Community understanding of the spiritual journey

Alone Together: 'The interrelation of personal solitudes'

A strong influence on the early development of Northumbria Community ethos came from the writings of the Cistercian monk Thomas Merton. In his preface to his book *Thoughts in Solitude*, Merton explains that,

> In the main these reflections on man's solitude before God, man's dialogue with God in silence, and the interrelation of our personal solitudes with one another, are for [him] essential to his own peculiar way of life.
>
> *Thomas Merton*

It seems to me that the sentence, 'the interrelation of our personal solitudes with one another' is as good an insight into the heart of Alone Together as we will find. Our solitude before God, and our dialogue with God in silence, constitutes the Alone for each one of us. But this is not an end in itself as Merton goes on to say: it is 'the interrelation of our personal solitudes with one another' that constitutes the Together. In order to gain an understanding of Northumbria Community as an interior monastic community of the heart, we must understand that we need to relate to each other in this way.

Although the expression of our way for living is diverse, we share core values, just as those in a family share DNA, so that underneath the richness of diversity the heart is the same. Seeking God is the 'one thing necessary' for all Companions in Community and having space to do this Alone strengthens the ties that bind us Together.

This is a key understanding of the Northumbria Community ethos and purpose. By the grace of God, each Companion can now understand that his or her solitude is shared: we are Alone Together.

Clarifying how we use the phrase
Alone Together

However, a little research will soon reveal that the phrase 'Alone Together' is used widely and far beyond the Northumbria Community, and is understood in many different ways, with both positive and negative connotations.

For example, one use that is decidedly cautionary is in the high-tech world of today's millennial generation and their constant use of smart phones and digital technology in every area of their lives. Recent research, into what is primarily a self-inflicted virtual reality isolation, confirms [that]:

> The alone together phenomenon is becoming a curse, creating real issues of stress, feelings of being overwhelmed, and the inability to form strong interpersonal relationships. In fact, from personal conversations and observation, I believe certain skills, particularly verbal and non-verbal communication, are being diminished in direct proportion to the time spent alone with our tech. And, whether you like it or not, the 'alone together' phenomenon is increasingly a cross generational issue affecting everyone and all aspects of our everyday lives and work environments.
>
> *Gaynor Strachan Chun*

Another, more bizarre example of a different understanding and usage was reported on the American cable news channel CNN on December 30, 2015 under the headline 'Couple caned for being Alone Together'.

> An unrelated man and woman who had been seen alone together were caned in public in Banda Aceh, Indonesia, for violating Sharia law, a police chief said. The form of Islamic law is enforced in a very strict way in the area, including prohibiting unmarried people of different genders from being alone together. A judge sentenced the two to caning.

The couple – whose offence involved merely being in 'close proximity' to each other – were university students studying in the same room.

Both of these rather unusual examples demonstrate a very different mind-set and perception when seen against the backdrop of our own usage of Alone Together. Our focus is on describing how Alone Together relates to significant aspects of the spiritual journey from the perspective of the Northumbria Community ethos.

Even so, we still need to clarify the central meaning of Alone Together as we use the term. Firstly, we need to say that it is not our intention to diminish or denigrate the awfulness of unwanted loneliness or isolation. Secondly, it would be both misleading and a misrepresentation, to interpret our phrase 'alone together' as simply loneliness or fellowship, or only as times when we are on our own as opposed to times when we are with others. It's much more than that – it is for the Northumbria Community a succinct way of describing the spirituality that is at the heart of our vocation and which we seek to live out in our daily lives.

This is because in the Northumbria Community, our spiritual journey is both inward and personal and thus Alone, and also outward and corporate and thus Together. Being Alone Together is an essential part of our Community's theology and vocation. Alone Together is inner journey stuff: for us Alone includes solitude, silence, prayer, hiddenness and contemplation, whilst Together includes intercession, community, hospitality, engagement and involvement.

Having said that, and especially as a geographically dispersed network, we understand that, at times, Alone Together can take on a slightly different meaning. There are times when Alone Together can take on the added understanding of Alone *and* Together, for example in our liturgies: 'As a Community Alone and Together we confess our sins...' We might see this extra layer of meaning in a prayer: 'May all Companions in Community, Alone and Together, know the blessing of God', or as an explanation of a theme 'in order to understand something deeper about who God is, who we are, and what our purpose is in the work of God in the world, alone and together.'

And when for instance, we are praying our daily Morning Office from *Celtic Daily Prayer,* we begin in the singular: 'One thing I have asked of the Lord...' but then the question and response 'Who is it that you seek? We seek the Lord our God...' is plural, referring to people together. Similarly, when in a group situation, we still say the liturgy as an individual alone, but we are saying it together with other individuals alone. For example, 'Christ as a light illumine and guide me ...' but as others, alone, voice the same prayer with us, we are alone together.

We can also speak of Alone *yet* Together, as when Companions and Friends live in different locations, often in different countries, as this highlights the sense of spiritual oneness and community of the heart. For example, our friends in the De Spil Community (Dutch for spindle or axis) are located in the village of Giessenburg, in the west of Holland. They gave us a helpful insight into this particular meaning, when a group of our Community folk visited them. One of the first things noted was the wording on the plaque attached to the fence next to the entrance gate. It said,

> 'We eat together, even if it isn't at one table'
> 'We live together, even if it isn't in one house'
> 'We pray together, even if it isn't in one chapel'

This summarises our own understanding, and is a helpful way to appreciate that, in becoming a Companion in the Northumbria Community, we are not simply joining a local expression, wherever it is. Rather we are joining a world wide Community – a community of the heart – and in doing so, we become the local expression wherever we live, wherever we gather. This reinforces the fact that for each Companion, in the way we see things, the way we operate, the way we live our Rule of Life – whatever context or cultural expression we find ourselves in – the way of life is relevant and real.

As we have seen, there are several valid usages of the phrase Alone Together, found in various walks of life, but, if we are to understand Alone Together in the context of Northumbria Community history and ethos, we must grasp a further crucial focus of meaning. We will explore this fully in the next chapter but it will help to set the scene with some historical context.

Community starts with the cell

Our Community's life and spirituality was founded on the Cell principle – the heart Alone with God. We didn't consciously begin with the Together, but with the Alone. Individuals sought God for themselves, all of them, in varying degrees, going through the inner experience of what Merton called 'monastic dread.' This, he says, is:

> the curious state of alienation and confusion ... the inner conflict which makes us guess that in order to be true to God and to ourselves we must break with the familiar, established and secure norms and go off into the unknown.
>
> *Thomas Merton*

This, often scary, sense of alienation and confusion was coupled with the joy of discovering that there were others going through the very same experience. We found that others were on the same faith journey, asking the same questions and expressing the same doubts. They expressed the same fears, sense of lostness and inner exile, but carried the same hopes in seeking God. We slowly realised that this was a vocation God had called many to live – so our response was 'Let's live it together! Let's explore this interior monasticism. Let's be open to discover a new way for living to support and sustain our continuing quest for a Northumbrian spirituality.'

This pattern is still on-going and is why as a dispersed Community, geographically distanced, we can be Alone in experiencing this monastic dread and yet Together with all those whose journey parallels our own as a community of the heart, wherever we are physically located.

So Community began, not as Community but as individual pioneers responding in vulnerability and originality to the call of God. The formative years of Community were like a journey without maps, characterised by risk taking and experimentation. As the founders pioneered and explored, following a vocation without knowing how it would appear or what it would look like in the future, a Community emerged around them – unplanned and spontaneous – as their pioneering drew others with a similar heart and a common commitment to the values and the way of life being worked out through their shared experiences. Out of this life actually being lived, with shared relationships and core values, a Rule of life was formed. This became the interpretive framework for the vocation and vision of all subsequent Companions in Community: a means of handing on the tradition.

So Community starts with the Cell – the heart alone with God. The Cell is the single-minded search for the one thing necessary to the monastic heart. In the Cell we learn to embrace all our lesser desires (both good and bad) with the one great desire, that is to love God with all our heart, soul, mind, and strength and to love our neighbour as our self.

For the Northumbria Community, the Cell is a reminder that every thing else in the spiritual life is secondary to seeking God for our self in the solitude of our own heart. To know God there must be a willingness to know self: to take responsibility for our own heart and journey, as no one can do it for us. We believe that, if we cultivate this as a discipline, it will gradually bring us to a greater understanding of both God-awareness and self-awareness. Then, in discovering who we are, and who God is, it will enable us to engage in the world around us passionately and realistically. As Thomas Merton aptly puts it:

> The more we are one with God, the more we are united with one another.
>
> *Thomas Merton*

So, one of the first things we each have to learn, in being part of Northumbria Community, is that we are alone. No one can seek God for us, be God for us, live our lives or make our decisions, be they Pastor, Priest or Pope. At times people, initially interested in our way for living but seeking a more pastoral, fellowship model, have become disillusioned in not fully understanding this. Therefore, in our Novitiate process we seek to address clearly this important aspect of the inner journey.

Proverbs 14:10 puts it well:

> The heart knows its own bitterness,
> and no stranger shares its joy

No one can give me to God except me – and no one can give you to God except you. We can encourage one another and be alongside each other, but in the end the only real gift I can give to another is who I really am, the gift of myself!

In other words, we each need to come to that place where we can say: I am only responsible for me, for my journey, for the times when my heart is alone before God. I cannot be anyone else; indeed it is wrong to want to be. I am me, I want to be the best me that I can be. As long as I want to be someone or something else, I'm off centre. I can't be Tom, Dick or Harriet any more than they can be me, but because Tom, Dick, and Harriet are on the same journey, seeking God and following the same Rule of Life, we are paradoxically alone together!

In describing this way of being Together in our Aloneness, the 4th century Egyptian monk Pachomius coined the phrase 'a Community of Hermits'. This is how, as a dispersed Community, geographically distanced, we can still be Alone Together.

It is as Franciscan Priest Richard Rohr explains:

> Who we are is all we finally have to give the world, and the only thing that God is asking of us. All the doing, as necessary and as good as it is, is just practice and preparation for the ultimate experience of just being.
>
> *Richard Rohr*

It is our ordinary, everyday lives that are usable for God: our person and our being, so that we don't have to be successful or effective, only available and vulnerable, teachable and faithful. God takes it all from there. We are all in the process of being and becoming. Those committed to seeking God as the one thing necessary in their lives know that this is a continual process – being and becoming a new person, wiser, more at home with ourselves, easier to live with, more contented, able to accept who we are with joy and not resignation.

These are the fruits of spiritual formation and growth on the inner journey of transformation. Being teachable and open to change is what keeps us alive.

Chapter 2

How does **Alone Together** *help us understand the nature of God?*

That God, being a Trinity of Persons in relationship, wants us to reflect his heart of love in relationship with each other

The Northumbria Community believes God is Trinity, that is, Persons in relationship. The profound truth is that we are made in His image and likeness. Our Christian faith and tradition tells us that it is God's purpose in and through Jesus Christ to work towards fully restoring that image and likeness in every expression of His Church. The early Celtic Northumbrian spirituality had a profound understanding of this. One of their prayers stated:

> God is Father, Son and Spirit. Therefore God is Three in One. Therefore God is Community. If we are made in the image of God, then we will find our fulfilment in Community (in relationships of love).

Our own Midday Office liturgy from *Celtic Daily Prayer* clearly confirms our belief in a Tri-unity of Three Persons stating:

> We believe and trust in God the Father Almighty.
> We believe and trust in Jesus Christ his Son.
> We believe and trust in the Holy Spirit.
> We believe and trust in the Three-in-One.

It is the nearest we come to having a statement of faith.

It is always good to remind ourselves, as Christians, that Community began in the heart of God; the self-sufficient God, who is love, is Community within Himself, and all Community flows from this. So, if we are to reflect the image and likeness of God – the Trinity of Three Persons – it follows that true spiritual community has to be a community of persons, and not a collection of individuals: each person uniquely alone and yet in relationship with others who are also uniquely alone, so that we are alone together.

This is why, in describing the nature of God as Trinity, we must emphasise that it is God in three persons and not three individuals. The difference is crucial. What makes me who I am and what makes you who you are is 'the mysterious uniqueness that defies any definition'. We each occupy a place that no one else can. As Rowan Williams says:

> The realm of the personal is that realm in which what I am, unique, mysterious and distinctive, comes into relation with what is unique, mysterious and distinctive in you. Each of us then makes the other yet more unique and mysterious and distinctive in the process of encounter.
>
> *Rowan Williams*

God is a communion of community, a God of mutual self-giving. And this has implications for us. Coming to Christian faith is entering into this love relationship between Father, Son and Holy Spirit. This is the ultimate welcome and befriending. It is also the ultimate homecoming. It is entering into the circle of love, mutuality and care of the Trinity that defines our identity, reconfigures our life of fear and insecurity and sustains a journey of growth in Christ-likeness and service to the world.

> This communion, this mutuality, this love, this welcome, we are to reflect in the communities of faith which seek to be a witness to the beauty of this God. Thus the doctrine of the Trinity is no dry-as-sawdust doctrine. It is a living statement of who God is and what God does and what we are to become as servants of the reign of God.
>
> *Charles R. Ringma*

As a Community we can affirm every day, Alone Together, the beginning of St Patrick's Breastplate hymn, 'I bind unto myself this day the strong Name of the Trinity'. It is a living awareness that God the Father is FOR us, God the Son is WITH us, and God the Holy Spirit is IN us:

> You, dear children, are from God and have overcome them, because the One who is in you is greater than the one who is in the world.
>
> *(1 John 4:4)*

That God deals with each of us as our unique self in the cell of our own hearts

As we have indicated, the Northumbria Community has drawn much from the desert monastic tradition, not least the advice of the Desert Fathers to 'go to your cell and your cell will teach you everything'. This was a succinct way of saying that the spiritual life is not about prescribing pat answers or techniques but an exhortation to just get on with life as it is. This is because life (spiritual or otherwise) is simply the next thing that happens, more often than not in the ordinary times and humdrum days that make up much of daily life.

The outworking of this for Companions in the Northumbria Community is that no matter what 'the next thing that happens' is for us, our commitment is to develop a rhythm of prayer that continues as we engage with work, resume unfinished tasks or simply potter about, and always to be prepared to go to the cell – to our inner heart alone with God.

Once there, we need, with courage, honesty and humility, to examine the thoughts, impulses, and emotions that we experience as the person we truly are, in order to discern from our actions and reactions, what is constructive and what is destructive in our seeking after God. Monastic teaching tells us that this is not mere navel-gazing or self-analysis; the whole point of the exercise is to prevent such introspection and obsession. It is, instead, a radical honesty with the inner self that is willing to be vulnerable, a way of letting things be seen, exactly as they are, before the God whose grace we believe to be all-sufficient.

Alessandro Pronzato puts it well when he writes that:

> If you therefore go to the [cell] to be rid of all the dreadful people and all the awful problems in your life, you will be wasting your time. You should go to the [cell] for a total confrontation with yourself. For one goes to the [cell] to see more and to see better. One goes to the [cell] especially to take a closer look at the things and people one would rather not see, to face situations one would rather avoid, to answer questions one would rather forget.
>
> *Alessandro Pronzato*

One of the first effects of going to the cell is the release of the energies of the unconscious, which gives rise to two different psychological states.

- The first state is exposure to the love of God, expressed and experienced in our personal development in the form of spiritual consolation. We experience God's mercy, grace and forgiveness in Christ through his work on the Cross.

- The second state is exposure to the sinfulness of humanity: experiencing our own human weakness through humiliating self-knowledge in the form of spiritual desolation. We encounter the false self, the dark side of our personality.

In this regard, the 17th century French scientist and philosopher Blaise Pascal comments:

> To know God without knowing our own wretchedness only makes for pride. Knowing our own wretchedness without knowing God makes only for despair. Knowing Jesus Christ provides the balance, because we find there both God and our own wretchedness.

> *Blaise Pascal, James M. Houston*

This dual awareness is what the Fathers called 'compunction' and is captured in the words of an old hymn

> Beneath the Cross of Jesus ... two wonders I confess;
> the wonder of His glorious love and my own worthlessness...

> *Elizabeth Clephane*

Another significant insight from Merton is contained in his essay entitled *The Cell*, where he discusses those seeking God who still crave what he calls:

> a fully recognisable and acceptable identity, a place in the church [over against those] travelling a way that is new and disconcerting because it has never been imagined by us before ... a way in which we seem to lose our identity and become nothing ... [This] obscure

life of the cell ... implies a kind of mysterious awakening to the fact that where we actually are is where we belong, namely in solitude, in the cell. Suddenly we see, 'this is it'.

Thomas Merton

Here we have described an all-consuming way for living that is authentic and real. This is it! We see it as where we belong! There can be no going back; having discovered this new way for living, there is no other way. It echoes our own Morning Office liturgy, 'To whom shall we go, you have the words of eternal life and we have believed and have come to know that you are the holy one of God'. Do you seek him with all your heart? Amen but Lord ... have mercy!

When we find ourselves in this situation, what is needed is coherence, hope and a pathway to follow. Our discovery as Northumbria Community is that this comes from an embracing of monastic values and vocation: a new monasticism that says 'Yes' to God by saying 'Yes' to Availability and Vulnerability as that pathway for living. It is this 'monastic' calling that we are seeking to respond to: to seek God for his own sake, to capture the heart of true monasticism, that is single-mindedness in seeking God.

We believe, as a Community, that it is as we discover a rhythm for our day that actually works in the ordinariness of everyday life and commitments and as we adopt a regular practice of going to the cell, that we will find what we need. We believe that this discipline will eventually teach us everything about the deeper meaning of our actions and reactions; it will nourish spiritual growth and bring us closer to the true humanity of Christ-likeness.

George Lings writes that:

'going to the cell' ... is of cardinal importance if today's Christians are to recover from the viruses of consumerism and dependency that are rife in church life and have crossed almost unnoticed from the deeply addictive western culture in which we live.

George Lings

God wants us to know Him as the 'one thing necessary' and seek Him for Himself alone whether in confidence or dread; in light or darkness

It will come as no surprise to readers thus far, when I say that one of the greatest discoveries for me in my own faith journey was the writings of Thomas Merton, a Cistercian Monk and a prolific author. Through his writings he has become a spiritual director to thousands across the world. His understanding of contemplative spirituality, not as external practices but as a monasticism of the heart, lived in the ordinariness of life, greatly influenced the Northumbria Community in its quest to understand a new monasticism as a vocational expression.

Quotations from many of his writings can be found in early documents of the Northumbria Community and in the early foundational lectures entitled *Internal Émigrés* held in the Anglican church of Old Bewick, North Northumberland, consecutively over the winter months of late 1991 and early 1992. These quotations were central to the ethos and spirituality being developed.

On a personal level, I remember, as a local church minister in a strongly conservative evangelical church, struggling to understand my own experience of the seeming loss of God's felt presence in my life. Most bewildering of all was the fact that, through this experience, my desire for God was still very real. On a family visit to The Grange, near Whittingham in Northumberland (the original Nether Springs), I mentioned this to John (my brother-in-law) and he said he had been reading Merton and proceeded to tell me about his teaching on the two types of darkness.

Up to that point I had only ever heard of one type of darkness and that was the darkness of sin, caused by our own wilful sin and wrong choices. Our relationship with God and other people begins to break down and we are ripe for capture by 'the world, the flesh and the devil.' The way out of this darkness is profoundly simple – 'we arise and go to the Father' and in repentance we confess our sins and receive forgiveness through the work of Jesus on the Cross.

According to Merton there is also a second type of darkness – the darkness of faith that has been likened to God going out of the room of our lives and, on his way out, switching off the light. We feel a general dryness and dissatisfaction with both our prayer life and our daily life. We experience 'numbness and dumbness' – no feeling, no explanation – only continual dryness in which God seems absent. Despite a desire for his love and a willingness to persevere in faith, we feel abandoned and miserable. This type of darkness is marked by a real fear that we are going backwards because in some way, either through personal fault or failure, we have offended God.

Merton was echoing the teaching of the sixteenth century Spanish Carmelite, poet and mystic St John of the Cross. He taught that this God-given 'Dark Night' is God calling our hearts to seek a deeper relationship with Him that is not dependent on the senses – on His felt presence – but on faith alone.

> Who among you fears the Lord and obeys the word of his servant?
> Let him who walks in the dark, who has no light, trust in the name of
> the Lord and rely on His God.
>
> *(Isaiah 50:10)*

John told me that this could be the explanation for my experience; that this experience is positive because it is not about loss of faith, or the literal absence of God, but a profound way of expressing faith in God and His real presence. Henri Nouwen called it 'the ever present absence of God'. This insight from Merton changed the whole direction of my life.

Going Deeper

Here we come back to the crucial meaning of Alone Together referred to in Chapter 1. To help us understand it, we need to expand on what Merton refers to as the 'inner experience of dread'. It is worth meditating upon this significant passage below, as it is an accurate description of what was happening to many in the formative years of the Northumbria Community's ethos and purpose.

The curious state of alienation and confusion of man in modern society is perhaps more bearable because it is lived in common, with the multitude of distractions and escapes – and also with opportunities for fruitful action and genuine Christian self-forgetfulness. But underlying all life is the ground of doubt and self-questioning which sooner or later must bring us face-to-face with the ultimate meaning of our life. This self-questioning can never be without a certain existential dread – a sense of insecurity, of lostness, of exile, of sin. A sense that one has somehow been untrue not so much to abstract moral or social norms but to one's own inmost truth. Dread, in this sense, is not simply a childish fear of retribution, or a naive guilt, a fear of violating taboos. It is the profound awareness that one is capable of ultimate bad faith with oneself and with others: that one is living a lie...

> The deep root of monastic 'dread' is the inner conflict which makes us guess that in order to be true to God and to ourselves we must break with the familiar, established and secure norms and go off into the unknown.
>
> *Thomas Merton*

This insight about the inner experience of monastic dread was a key factor in understanding the development of the Northumbria Community. In seeking God alone and discovering others seeking God alone, who were on the same inner journey and experiencing the same darkness and dread, we also discovered a togetherness as a community of the heart. We were Alone Together in learning 'How then shall we live?', in understanding 'How shall we sing the Lord's song in a strange land', and applying this as lived wisdom in the ordinary roles and responsibilities of daily life.

In the early days of Northumbria Community the concept of monastic dread helped us to understand our reaction to the massive changes in social, cultural, ecclesiastical, psychical, and moral spheres that have been ushered in with a post-modern outlook. It enabled us to put a name to the inner experience itself. We found that the words lostness, exile and darkness helped us to describe what was happening in us and around us.

We also found that we already had a way for living with our dread, through our Rule of Life and Rhythm of daily prayer. These worked to bring some coherence in ordinary, day-to-day living in the midst of life's uncertainties, doubts, absurdities, and contradictions. Further help came through the discovery of authentic examples of a lived spirituality in Bonhoeffer's *Life Together*, in desert spirituality, and 'dark night' theology in the context of the Celtic monasticism of Northumbria.

Many others, also struggling spiritually, mentally and emotionally, and often without knowing why, came – and continue to make their way – to the Nether Springs (our Mother House) or find help in our resources and teaching. Nether Springs was opened as a residential centre, rooted in the spirituality of Northumbria, to provide a place where we could be ourselves and explore and research this call of God. It was somewhere we could be free to seek God for Himself and get to know our own hearts. At the same time, it provided a safe space for others to join us in their own search for God. We call each of these seekers an internal émigré: one who has fled or is fleeing from upheaval and inner chaos, seeking a new way for living. This has been, and often still is, a common experience of the inner journey to varying degrees for the whole of our Community.

A further insight from Thomas Merton on the inner aspects of Alone Together spirituality is that:

> The monastic life demands first of all a profound understanding and acceptance of solitude ... the full affirmation of one's identity ... the complete acceptance of oneself as willed by God and of one's lot as given by God.
>
> *Thomas Merton*

That last phrase – 'of one's lot as given by God' – is the key here. We need to accept this reality: that whatever we are going through in the angst of aloneness that comes from a loss of meaning in regard to our faith, and however seemingly unshakable is the uncertainty surrounding our experience of dread, dark night, alienation and sense of exile, it is all God given!

We can gain a deeper understanding of the different aspects of this God-given experience by looking at how it was described by three very different men: Leo Tolstoy, Parker J. Palmer and Henri Nouwen.

Leo Tolstoy, the 19th century Russian novelist, describes this feeling of dread very well in his book *My Confession*. He writes:

> My heart was oppressed by a tormenting feeling, which I cannot describe otherwise than as a searching after God. This search was not an act of my reason, but a feeling, and I say this advisedly, because it was opposed to my way of thinking; it came from the heart. It was a feeling of dread, of orphanhood, of isolation amid things all apart from me, and of hope in a help I knew not from whom.
>
> *Leo Tolstoy*

As he continued to seek God, with his need to find significance and purpose in his life, he eventually found that perseverance in prayer had an effect.

> He is, I said to myself. I had only to admit that for an instant to feel that life re-arose in me, to feel the possibility of existing and the joy of it ... I only really live when I feel and seek Him. What more, then, do I seek? A voice seemed to cry within me, 'This is He, He without whom there is no life. To know God and to live are one. God is life.'
>
> *Leo Tolstoy*

> Anyone who's been in personal pain – who has suffered depression, for example, as I have – has to learn that the only way out of inner darkness is to go down into it and find out what's there. You have to come to terms with what's in the darkness before you can come through to the other side. I can make a pretty good case that our culture is in a state of depression, which is a hard and unpleasant place to be. But it is also a place from which the courage to change

can start to emerge. This requires the guts to go into the darkness
instead of pretending it isn't there.

Parker J. Palmer

Everything came crashing down – my self-esteem, my energy to live
and work, my sense of being loved, my hope for healing, my trust in
God ... everything. Here I was, a writer about the spiritual life, known
as someone who loves God and gives hope to people, flat on the
ground and in total darkness.

Henri Nouwen

These stories remind us that Christian tradition has long recognised that
the road of faith is not always well lit. Coming to terms with the darkness
is part of the Christian journey because the darkness of faith is God given
and full of purpose – to teach us to put our security in God and not in
securities themselves. God takes seriously our desire for him.

I will give you treasures of darkness ... so you may know that I am the
Lord.

(Isaiah 45:3)

Our Day 3 meditation from *Celtic Daily Prayer Book 1: The Journey
Begins*, reminds us of the way forward – living in the real world, with all
its associated horrors and nightmares, but doing so with a creative tension
that recognises both protest and trust, fear and hope as valid expressions
of faith:

The cry to God as Father in the New Testament is not a calm
acknowledgement of a universal truth about God's abstract
Fatherhood; it is the child's cry out of a nightmare ... a cry of outrage,
fear, shrinking away, when faced with the horror of the world yet not
simply or exclusively protest but trust as well. Abba Father! All things
are possible to Thee.

Rowan Williams

Chapter 3

What does this mean for us as a Community and our way of being?

We are covenanted alone together with God and each other as a Community

As our Rule of Life reminds us, we need to be a Community willing to reform itself, especially as our growth and development has been substantial over these past 15 years. Now with second and third generations, the one constant has been our heart, our Rule, our ethos – still bringing together those inspired by the same spirit of adventure and vocational expression. This shared spirituality means that wherever we are, whoever we are, whatever we are, there is a recognisable pattern to be seen in the way we live our lives in the everyday. Despite our diversity, the ways we approach life – our attitudes, actions, and values – have real similarities because we share the same vows to the same Rule of Life of Availability and Vulnerability before God and others. It is the family likeness of shared DNA. God within is shaping and moving us to express God without in an ongoing process of daily discernment and decision making within our own unique setting.

This whole concept reminds us that the root meaning of covenant comes from the Latin *con venire*, literally a coming together. It is a bond, entered into voluntarily by two (or more) parties, by which each pledges to do something for the other and share the process of determining what rights and responsibilities are needed for a common understanding of the agreement entered into.

The supreme example of this, of course, is the shared commitment to loving-kindness and steadfast loyalty of the people of God that we read about again and again in the Bible. When the covenant God says, 'I shall be your God, you shall be my people' (Jeremiah 31:33), He expresses clearly what it means to say 'Yes' in coming together with Him and with others.

This understanding of covenant is so important that it may be helpful to briefly mention what we don't mean by covenant before emphasising what we do mean, in order that we may have a common understanding of our shared vocation – uniquely alone yet covenanted together.

- Our meaning is not that of a contract as in a legally binding business agreement for goods or services rendered or as in a deed of covenant where we agree to pay monies to a charity. Such contracts involve a give and take arrangement that carry legal obligations where penalties exist for breaking the contract. More often than not these contracts are entered into with an attitude of 'I will do my part only as long as you do your part'.

- Our meaning is not that of a creed, as in *credo* meaning I believe. These statements of faith and doctrine are formal confessions that carry authority from a hierarchy. Even with the best of intentions creeds tend to be exclusive, requiring that unless and until you believe exactly as I believe, we can't come together in heart. It follows that they are often static, legalistic, and divisive.

- Our meaning is that of Companionship. This rightly emphasises that the heart of covenant is distinctly relational, not merely propositional or contractual. It is shared vocation: a life lived with a common purpose and mutual intention. To use Bonhoeffer's term, we are 'banded together' to explore 'a new type of monasticism' as Companions in Community under a common Rule of Life.

Both contract and creed can be impersonal – simply a unity of cooperation to achieve a common goal – whereas covenant is personal, a unity of persons that can't be described in functional terms alone, hence Companions in Community.

The difference is crucial because a contract can be ripped up and discarded; a creed can be dismissed as no longer relevant. But this can't be done with a covenant because it is so much more than a sheet of paper or a set of principles. It is shared personhood and it is this sharing of each other's person – a community of the heart – that is the covenant relationship we share within the Northumbria Community.

Community is a gift from God, and in receiving this gift, we discover that we are committed to one another through a common commitment to follow Jesus. Our response has been: Yes to God, Yes to a Way for Living, Yes to Availability and Vulnerability, which is a Yes to Community.

We discover further that this gift is from One who has already said 'Yes' to us; we are covenanted together because we are each covenanted to God to follow our Way for Living. For the Northumbria Community, covenant relationship is not simply the friendship of a club or the team spirit of a sport or the acquaintance of a business venture but an inner awareness of coming home; of belonging Alone Together as Companions in Community.

It follows that one of the marks of Companions in Community is this awareness that covenant is reciprocal; I have something to give, but I also have something to receive. I give myself as a person to the whole and I am bonded together with everyone else who gives himself or herself as a person to the whole, and we all draw from the gift of persons who are wonderfully diverse and different from everyone else. We are Alone Together, covenanted together because we are each covenanted to God.

We all need both enclosure (Alone) and encounter (Together). This is the genius of our corporate identity – the Alone mediated through the Together and the Together mediated through the Alone – wherever we live and work.

Covenant means that we have been called to come together in heart and vocation, even though we are geographically dispersed. So that, wherever we are, our common purpose is centred in relational values – to seek God as the one thing necessary and to know self, so as to learn how we can better live with others, and serve the world of our influence, (however seemingly insignificant it is to us), in the ordinariness of who we are, doing the best we can to be an expression of Christ in the world.

Covenanted together within the love of Christ we share a common heart for Northumbria and a commitment to wander for the love of Christ wherever the Father leads.

We are both unintentional and intentional as a Community

One of the many characteristics that makes the Northumbria Community distinctive is that, in its expression of life as Alone Together, it has a mixture of unintentional and intentional aspects of being Community.

Our Community has always been a dispersed group in the sense that we have never intentionally sought to be a Community where every person belonging to us lived under one roof sharing a common life and a common purse. We live scattered in different places and apart from one another. Now (in 2018) we have hundreds of people living as Companions throughout the UK, Europe, and other places across the world, who are anything from 50 or 100 miles, to several thousand miles, away from the Mother House.

The Nether Springs, as our Mother House, has always sought to be a sign of the Community's monastic heart, a symbol of hope in a fragmented world. It is a reminder to the wider Community of the need to balance prayer that is quiet and contemplative with a faith that is active and contagious in expressing our Rule of Life as a different way for living. It is a school of the Lord's service, inspiring hope, encouraging and informing through living the values of heart, home, and hospitality. The life at the Mother House, through the ever-changing team and stream of visitors, constantly reflects and represents this ongoing exploration, emphasising that, when we become a Companion in Community, we join with the whole Community of Companions worldwide, not just with a focused local expression. This is why it is right to say that we are not, and never have been, an intentional, physical, lived Community in one place!

The unintentional nature of our Community is also seen in the unique journey that each of us makes alone with God in the cell. When we say Yes to our vocation of Availability and Vulnerability, no one else can do this for us and no one shares that moment with us except God.

But, by definition, Together has to mean intentional Community for those who have committed to our worldwide community of the heart and embraced our Way for Living in all aspects of life. When we enter the novitiate process and become a Companion in Community, we are saying Yes to the same way for living being shared by others who have also said Yes to our Rule of Life. Thus wherever we live; we are living Alone Together.

Alone Together relates to the whole of our lives since it is about doing and about being. In other words, whatever we do, we do it as the person we are: our personhood (mind, emotions, body, spirit, will) is an integrated whole. We are the same person going to work, cooking a meal, reading the Bible, mowing the lawn, shouting at the kids, saying our prayers, watching the TV, laughing, crying, worrying, frightened, bored, guilty, excited, angry, sad – whatever! Authentic spirituality touches and influences every part of our lives and every part of our lives touches and influences our spirituality. So whether we are alone with God, or sharing together in a collective expression of Community, we are living Alone Together as an authentic God-given, way of life.

> We have to keep in mind that community, like solitude, is primarily a quality of the heart ... community does not necessarily mean being physically together. We can well live in community while being physically alone. In such a situation, we can act freely, speak honestly, and suffer patiently, because of the intimate bond of love that unites us with others even when time and place separate us from them. The community of love stretches out not only beyond the boundaries of countries and continents but also beyond the boundaries of decades and centuries.
>
> *Henri Nouwen*

We live vocationally alone together as Companions in Community

I recall, some years ago, taking a three-day retreat at the Community of the Transfiguration in Roslin near Edinburgh. I had visited scores of times for a day of solitude and spiritual direction but this time I wanted to experience the actual and be no different from the way the monks lived. So I was put in a 6′ x 4′ hut; it was very cold and extremely basic with lots of spiders wanting to cosy up. I confess that it didn't take long for me to want to go home to my nice warm, comfortable bed. I didn't, as I sheepishly pondered the fact that the monks had lived this way for years. Why? The simple but profound answer was because it was the call of God; it was their vocational expression and way of life. They were committed to seeking and serving God in that place – whatever! Visiting the Community at Roslin was such a personal challenge! I always left with new resolve to seek, love and serve God, having witnessed such a supreme example of authentic living!

We cannot will ourselves into a vocation. By definition, a vocation calls a man or woman out of his or her current existence and into a new one. A vocation is acknowledged only through the prayerful process of discernment. It is never a pick n' mix lifestyle choice – saying in effect, I'll try this and if it doesn't work, I'll try something else. That is living with a consumer mentality, with 'I, my, me' at the centre, as a spiritual gypsy, flitting from place to place for no other reason than to gratify our own needs. The crucial difference is that in any true vocation, God is the one who does the choosing!

Let me highlight some Community teaching that will help us in discerning that difference. Imagine the difference between a vacation and a vocation!

- VACATION – To be a tourist on holiday is no bad thing. It is supportive to life in bringing rest and refreshment but it is peripheral and not an everyday occurance. It's largely a matter of the mind, bringing choices that we are in control of. We decide where we go and what we do. It is part of the outer journey, the landscape of the land. It is saying 'this is OK, but it's not me, it's not where I live, I'm a visitor and I must move on'.

- VOCATION – A pilgrim on vocation is very different. Vocation is integral to life and central to its everydayness. It's largely a matter of the heart in that God is in control of where we go and what we do. It is part of the inner journey, the landscape of the heart. It is a definite commitment to a way of life. Vocation is finding your identity in being who you are, who you are called to be, (vocare means 'to call') so that all you do comes from this. It is saying 'this is me, this is where I belong, this is home, this is who I am. I need to stay, even when I don't want to'.

This discernment is so important because to be part of Northumbria Community has to involve a vocational understanding that is real. A Companion understands that Northumbria Community is about a way for living internalised in the heart rather than a way for knowing indoctrinated in the mind. To really grasp this is crucial!

Paul Cullity, a long-term Companion, helpfully described it as the difference between a grocery list and a stew – they have the same ingredients, but are very different in nature and purpose. A tourist on vacation can gather knowledge that can be listed but a pilgrim with a vocation gathers wisdom that is simply lived. Many mentoring or apprentice programmes seem to centre on the grocery list approach – these are the ingredients, this is what you need to know or believe, please tick the relevant boxes in the checklist. Ideally, Companions in Community are those who have not only heard the message of our vocation but who are the message of our vocation. For them, the ingredients have blended together and been taken in to nourish and sustain themselves and others.

Our novitiate process has to be more about becoming a participant as each personal story is embraced by the one story that is the vocational expression of Northumbria Community. For us this involves a constant reference to the three questions: Who is it that you seek? How then shall we live? How do we sing the Lord's song…? That's why we have called those in full participation, Companions.

The word 'Companion' comes from an ancient Latin tradition. In the Roman army it was common practice for people of the same language and culture to live close to one another and share the ordinary, common things of life. The leaders identified their men by the group they ate with and, in time, the phrase cum panis, literally meaning 'with bread, or bread together' came into general use to describe those who belonged together and shared the same journey, eventually giving us the words 'company', and 'companion'. As Companions of Northumbria Community we share in the same spiritual food each day through the liturgy of the Daily Office. This is our calling, our vocational expression Alone Together.

> For wisdom is God Himself, living in us, revealing Himself to us. Life reveals itself to us only in so far as we live it.
>
> *Thomas Merton*

We are called to live a new monasticism alone together

New monasticism has to do with turning toward God in the midst of the world, not separating from the world in order to find God. The world is very much within us, albeit in different forms, and in the lives of all that we meet.

Northumbria Community is a fulfilment of the new monasticism spoken of prophetically by Thomas Merton in the last book he wrote before his untimely death:

> The purpose of monastic renewal and reform is to find ways in which monks and sisters can remain true to their vocation by deepening and developing it in new ways, not merely sacrificing their lives to bolster up antique structures, but channelling their efforts into the creation of new forms of monastic life, new areas of contemplative experience.
>
> *Thomas Merton*

We discovered the root meaning of 'monastic' is being single-minded in seeking God, describing a person united within herself, a person with a single gaze, a single desire. The one thing necessary is to be available to God, seeking Him in the cell of your own heart, with an attitude of inner vulnerability because it is a continual confrontation with the Cross, with self, with sin, with the wrong of the world, while all the time simply getting on with life as it is. This life may or may not be carried out in the company of others, (the monastic tradition has embraced both), but the focus is clearly on a continual conversion, a constant returning to God. It was a way of life lived within, or outside of, a monastery. In the 4th century, two rightly famous contemporaries developed different aspects of monastic life; Antony of Egypt developed the Anchorites, who were hermits, living in isolation, whereas Pachomius developed the Cenobites, living alone together as a community of hermits.

The monastic life is a life lived from the inside out, not from the outside in. Many in the Church are still attached to externals: ritual, doctrine etc.

An example of the outside in approach can be seen in a recent email I received from a genuine enquirer about our Community:

> Please can you tell me if you celebrate Easter and Christmas, as they both came from the Roman Catholic church, and what Bible version do you read from? Do you preach the Pre Trib Rapture? What are your views on Daniel's 70 weeks which Christ fulfilled fully? The Lord has opened up our eyes to many lies, and we are wary, to what church we join. Because we don't want to be entangled with anything to do with the Roman Catholic Church, and her festivals, and false doctrine.

I replied that, while we genuinely respect his views and honour his spiritual journey, as a Community, we have Roman Catholics, Orthodox, and Protestants in all its many varieties as Companions in Community because we believe that in all of this we are first and foremost called to know God in Christ, the Source of all life. I went on to say that it seems to us that Anglican Archbishop Michael Ramsay got the balance right when he said that he 'wished to understand and even learn from theological views which were not his own, while at the same time commending a generous and tolerant orthodoxy'.

For us, the inner life with God, seen in all aspects of our own lives, is our motivating factor, and not our external circumstances. That's why the constant theme of our heart, our 'reason to be', is Psalm 27:

> One thing I ask of the Lord,
> this is what I seek:
> that I may dwell in the house of the Lord
> all the days of my life;
> To behold the beauty of the Lord
> and to seek Him in His temple.

We renew our vow to seek God, as the one thing necessary, every day as we pray Morning and Evening Office: 'One thing I ask of the Lord; one thing I seek'. Then we can offer the fruit of our life in everyday ordinariness with all who come our way, asking with them 'Who is it that you seek? 'How then shall we live? How shall we sing the Lord's song in a strange land?

The Rt Revd. John Pritchard, former Bishop of Oxford and one of our Community Visitors, wrote about the Church in general stating that:

> One of our greatest needs is to provide 'third spaces' (neither church nor home) where people can explore, reflect, observe for a while, and then approach in their own time.
>
> *John Pritchard*

In a conversation with the Community leaders he went on to say that:

> The Northumbria Community occupies an interesting 'Third Space', which is not the long established denominations and their traditional monastic communities, and nor is it a newer form of church (as in fresh expressions) or newer 'new monastic' communities. One of the gifts of the Northumbria Community to the body of Christ today is that it is rooted through its thirty years of exploration, and yet at the same time it is also still seen to be experimental and prophetic.

This is very insightful as we are still exploring and not trying to create church as a fresh expression. Traditional church, the fresh expressions and emergent churches are all influences. We are clearly a new monastic community but not in the limited sense of simply being part of a movement. We don't align ourselves to new monasticism as an organised, structured, controlled movement. Rather we believe that we are better defined by the prophetic words of Dietrich Bonhoeffer writing to his brother Karl Friedrich in 1935:

> The restoration of the Church must surely come from a new kind of monasticism, which will have only one thing in common with the old, a life lived without compromise according to the Sermon on the Mount in the following of Jesus. I believe the time has come to gather people together for this.
>
> *Mary Bosanquet*

And by the prophetic words of William Stringfellow writing in 1973 and describing the characteristics of the 'church' of the future as those who are:

Dynamic and erratic, audacious and immature, committed if not altogether coherent. Ecumenically open and often experimental, visible here and there, now and then but unsettled institutionally, most of all – enacting a fearful hope for society ... which is virtually monastic in character.

William Stringfellow

The Northumbria Community is exploring this 'third space', which is described elsewhere as the gap between the internal and the external. This is important because to stress one against the other means we either become consumed by the inner journey and what is happening within us to the neglect of the outer journey or we are so taken up with the events and happenings of the outer journey that we pay little or even no attention to the inner journey. This 'third space' is where we live the questions, where we are 'purposefully lost, deliberately uncertain and resolutely confused' – a place of safety on both the inner journey and the outer journey.

Northumbria Community is a prophetic re-imagining voice alongside the church rather than within it. It is important for the Northumbria Community to operate alongside the church rather than inside any denomination because if we were inside we would have to be under the authority of that denomination or hierarchy. We are still exploring, still asking the questions, and still learning what it means to be a geographically dispersed new monastic community. Yes, we honour and respect and indeed learn from traditional and fresh expressions of church but we are following our own call of God to:

Sow righteousness for yourselves, reap the fruit of unfailing love, and break up your unploughed ground; for it is time to seek the LORD, until he comes and showers his righteousness on you.

(Hosea 10:12)

In his book, *Redeeming the Time,* Thomas Merton, in discussing the more scattered nature of new monastic expressions, states that the monastic life exists 'not in order to become part of a hierarchical institution with rigid rules and complex ceremonies, but in order to seek God.'

A new monastic, he says, would be 'distinguished from the world' only by his humility and dedication, and his 'fidelity to life and to truth, rather than by his garments, [and] the cloister in which he lives…' This 'monasticity of heart' was 'not merely a conventional notion of "an interior life for the layman" but the idea of a lay-monk … without the benefit of distinguishing marks and outward forms, called to deepen his monastic vocation…' through a commitment to solitude and prayer, simplicity and work, as spiritual disciplines in the ordinariness of life.

Thomas Merton

Chapter 4

Alone Together: Conclusion

Henri Nouwen helps us finalise our subject matter when he writes:

> When we have heard God's voice in our solitude we will also hear it in our life together. When we have heard him in our fellow human beings, we will also hear him when we are with him alone. Whether in solitude or community, whether alone or with others, we are called to live obedient lives, that is, lives of unceasing prayer – 'unceasing' not because of the many prayers we say but because of our alertness to the unceasing prayer of God's Spirit within and among us.

> *Henri Nouwen*

These words are echoed by Dietrich Bonhoeffer when, in writing about community, he states that:

> A Christian fellowship lives and exists by the intercession of its members for one another, or it collapses. I can no longer condemn or hate a brother for whom I pray; no matter how much trouble he causes me ... This is a happy discovery for the Christian who begins to pray for others.

> *Dietrich Bonhoeffer*

These words from Bonhoeffer's *Life Together* remind us of a crucial, perhaps indispensable, spiritual discipline required in the outworking of Alone Together that is required in building community; it is praying and interceding for one another and the world on a daily basis. Of course this isn't only addressing the importance of prayer but the whole issue of relationships in community. In *Life Together* we are reminded that, in Christ, we belong together. It is a divine reality that is not dependent upon experience. We are bound to one another because of what God has done for us in Christ, not because of shared interests or common understandings.

Christian community is a gift of God. It is not an ideal that we must work to realise; it is rather a reality created by God in Christ in which we may participate. In Christ, we are invited, more like summoned, to move beyond the boundaries of our individual lives into the shared reality of Christian community. There is a radical togetherness that Bonhoeffer was advocating. One of the ways in which we can express our togetherness is to pray for one another. To do so is to quickly discover that in our

Community there is a kaleidoscope of callings, contexts, passions and concerns for which we, alone together, are invited to pray and intercede.

This passage captures a core value of the Northumbria Community: that living for God in the 'daily round and common task' by cultivating a prayerful awareness – of God, of self, of the world around us – is essential to any understanding of a new monastic spirituality. Put simply: prayer is life and life is prayer. This describes an attitude of heart that is rooted in the reality of what is. It is a simple willingness to be open and attentive to God in the routine of the everyday.

At its heart is the proven wisdom of both Scripture and Tradition that urges us to be committed to the daily discipline of living a day at a time. We say this every morning in our Office, 'This day be within and without me' and it's one of God's great gifts to us – a new beginning each and every day.

> Because of the Lord's great love we are not consumed, for his compassions never fail. They are new every morning; great is your faithfulness. I say to myself, 'The Lord is my portion, therefore I will wait for him'.
>
> *(Lamentations 3:22- 24)*

This commitment to living our lives in manageable portions, of having a continuity of new and fresh beginnings, is essential to our sanity.

Drawing from monastic values and spiritual disciplines, we seek a workable pattern for our life a day at a time. With the help of our Daily Office, we seek to live in the day in which we find ourselves. Life can't ever be uniform, as it is clearly different for all of us, but the principle of adopting a workable rhythm to our lives is vital: being, working, sleeping, praying, questioning, relaxing, etc. are all needed to give a healthy balance. The Northumbria Community encourages people to adopt such a daily rhythm that works for them in their own situations and circumstances.

It is a framework that helps us, naturally and gradually, incorporate reminders of God's presence into the life we already live. Repetition and association are key elements in sustaining a spiritual life; it's not so much about adding disciplines to an already busy life but becoming conscious of God in what we are already doing. Our part is to remain available, to listen, to observe, to act, to be. This enables us to remain spiritually alive, with a conscious God awareness, deliberately approaching daily life with the intention of knowing God, and so cultivating our disciplines and habits to that end.

Returning to Bonhoeffer, we note that for him Christian life was this healthy tension between solitude and sociality – life alone and life together as essential parts of one whole. He too understood that we each need both enclosure and encounter.

Each by itself has profound perils and pitfalls. One who wants fellowship without solitude plunges into the void of words and feelings, and the one who seeks solitude without fellowship perishes in the abyss of vanity, self-infatuation and despair.

If a person cannot bear to be alone and craves community solely as an antidote to loneliness then they miss the opportunities to listen to God in the silence of their solitude.

Bonhoeffer states this is because 'you cannot escape from yourself; for God has singled you out'. God has called you, and you alone can respond as you. Christian spirituality is not group therapy as there are things only you can do. Therefore 'let [those] who cannot be alone beware of community'. But, he says, 'the reverse is also true', whoever cannot stand being in community should 'beware of being alone'. Solitude does not lead to more solitude but to community, to hospitality, how to better live with others. Part of our calling is to be in relationship with one another. The call of Christ is to you alone but you must live that aloneness with others; because 'the Church is the Church only as it exists for others'.

We are called to be available to God and to others, therefore we need to cultivate the spiritual disciplines to free us to reflect in silence in the cell – the heart alone with God – to open our hearts to God in hospitality, to welcome him into our lives, to listen for his voice, to hear his heartbeat for the world.

Northumbria Community stands or falls by how much each Companion is engaging with the Rule of Life as their vocational expression in the everyday ordinariness of life, taking seriously the embracing of a way for living, and the reality of the inner journey. It also matters how each of us commits to 'mission' in our sphere of influence as well as to daily prayer, financial support and the commonality of living the questions.

We want to encourage Companions, Friends and seekers to accept that uncertainty, constant change and creative chaos can be embraced as friends.

We exist to provide Companionship, Coherence and Community on the journey, not only for believers feeling isolated by the crises of faith in a changing society but also for all who recognise that we need to explore new ways of being Church. We acknowledge as a Community that we are still pioneering, and therefore pilgrims not settlers, willing to make mistakes, getting it wrong, living a messy spirituality of incompleteness and unfinished-ness, knowing that through it all, we are Alone Together.

Acknowledgements

Text: Trevor Miller

Page 6:
Copyright © Thomas Merton, 1975, *Thoughts in Solitude,* Burns & Oates, an imprint of Bloomsbury Publishing Plc.

page 7:
Gaynor Strachan Chun, *The Curse of the 'Alone Together' Phenomenon* LinkedIn.com Article 29 September 2015

page 10:
Copyright © Thomas Merton, 1969, *The Climate of Monastic Prayer,* Burns & Oates, an imprint of Bloomsbury Publishing Plc.

Page 11:
Thomas Merton, *New seeds of Contemplation,* copyright © 1961 by The Abbey of Gethsemani, Inc. Reprinted by permission of New Directions Publishing Corp.

Page 12: Richard Rohr, source untraced.

Page 14:
Northumbria Community, *Celtic Spirituality – A Beginner's Guide* <https://www.northumbriacommunity.org/articles/celtic-spirituality-a-beginners-guide> accessed 30 April 2018

Page 15:
Rowan Williams, *Silence and Honeycakes* (Lion Publishing: Oxford, 2003)

Page 15:
Charles R. Ringma, *Hear the Heartbeat with Henri Nouwen* (SPCK: London, 2006). Used with permission.

Page 16:
Alessandro Pronzato, *Meditations on the Sand* (St. Paul Publications: 1982)

Page 17:
Blaise Pascal, James M. Houston, *The Mind on Fire: Faith for the Skeptical and Indifferent* (Victor Books: Colorado Springs, 2006)

Page 17:
Elizabeth Clephane, *Beneath the Cross of Jesus*, 1868

Page 17-18:
Copyright © Thomas Merton, 1997, *Solitude and Love of the World,* Burns & Oates, an imprint of Bloomsbury Publishing Plc.

Page 18:
George Lings, *Encounters on the Edge 29: Northumbria Community: Matching Monastery and Mission* (Church Army: Sheffield, 2009)

Page 21:
Copyright © Thomas Merton, 1969, *The Climate of Monastic Prayer,* Burns & Oates, an imprint of Bloomsbury Publishing Plc.

Page 22:
Thomas Merton, *Contemplation in a World of Action* (Image Books: New York, 1973). Used with permission of The Merton Legacy Trust.

Page 23:
Leo Tolstoy, *My Confession* (Thomas Y. Crowell: New York, 1887)

Page 23-24:
Parker J. Palmer, 'Leadership and the Inner Journey' in *Leader to Leader* Volume 18, (Wiley: Hoboken NJ, Fall 2001). Copyright © by The Leader to Leader Institute.

Page 24:
Henri Nouwen, *The Inner Voice of Love: A Journey Through Anguish To Freedom* (DLT: London, 1997)

Page 24:
Rowan Williams, *The Wound of Knowledge,* 2nd revised edition (DLT: London, 1990)

Page 30:
Henri Nouwen, *Making All Things New* (Gill and MacMillan: Dublin, 1982)

Page 33:
Copyright © Thomas Merton, 1975, *Thoughts in Solitude,* Burns & Oates, an imprint of Bloomsbury Publishing Plc.

Page 34:
Copyright © Thomas Merton, 1969, *The Climate of Monastic Prayer,* Burns & Oates, an imprint of Bloomsbury Publishing Plc.

Page 36:
John Pritchard, *Why go to Church? A Little Book of Guidance* (SPCK: London, 2015)

Page 36:
Mary Bosanquet, *The Life & Death of Dietrich Bonhoeffer* (Hodder & Stoughton: London, 1968)

Page 37:
William Stringfellow, *An Ethic for Christians and Other Aliens in a Strange Land* (Word Books: Waco, TX, 1979). Used by permission of Wipf and Stock Publishers. www.wipfandstock.com

Page 38:
Thomas Merton, *Redeeming the Time* (Burns & Oates: London, 1966). Used with permission of The Merton Legacy Trust.

Page 40:
Henri Nouwen, *Making All Things New* (Gill and MacMillan: Dublin, 1982)

Page 40:
Dietrich Bonhoeffer, *Life Together* (SCM Press: London, 1954)

For more information about the Northumbria Community please contact:

Northumbria Community
Nether Springs
Croft Cottage
Acton Home Farm
Felton
Northumberland
NE65 9NU

office@northumbriacommunity.org

+44 (0)1670 787645

www.northumbriacommunity.org

To see our resources including *Celtic Daily Prayer,* published by Collins and now available in two volumes:

Celtic Daily Prayer Book 1: The Journey Begins
ISBN 9780008123024

and

Celtic Daily Prayer Book 2: Farther Up and Farther In
ISBN 9780008100193

please visit our online shop:

www.northumbriacommunity.org/shop